MOJO DEEP DIVE

FOR ADVANCED PROFESSIONALS

LIAM HENRY JR

TABLE OF CONTENTS

Preface: Diving Deep into Mojo

Welcome to *Mojo Deep Dive for Advanced Professionals*

Mojo, a modern and powerful web framework built on Perl, offers a rich set of features for building high-performance and scalable web applications. This book is designed to guide you through the intricacies of Mojo, delving into advanced techniques and best practices that will elevate your development skills.

Whether you're a seasoned Perl developer or a newcomer to Mojo, this book aims to provide you with a comprehensive understanding of the framework's capabilities. From mastering asynchronous programming and networking to exploring advanced template features and database integration, you'll discover the full potential of Mojo.

Throughout the book, we'll present real-world examples and practical exercises to reinforce your learning. You'll also gain insights into the latest developments in the Mojo ecosystem, ensuring that you're equipped with the knowledge to build cutting-edge applications.

We hope that this book will serve as a valuable resource for advanced Mojo developers, helping you to unlock the full power of this versatile framework. Happy coding!

Chapter 1: Mojo Fundamentals Revisited

1.1 A Quick Recap of Mojo's Core Concepts

Mojo is a modern, high-performance web framework built on top of Perl. It provides a clean and intuitive API for building web applications, network protocols, and more. Here are some of its core concepts:

1. Mojo::Application:

The foundation of a Mojo application.

Handles the event loop, request/response processing, and routing.

2. Mojo::Router:

Used to define routes and associate them with handlers.

Routes are typically defined using regular expressions.

3. Mojo::Request:

Represents an incoming HTTP request.

Provides access to headers, parameters, and body content.

4. Mojo::Response:

Represents an outgoing HTTP response.

Allows you to set headers, status codes, and body content.

5. Mojo::UserAgent:

A class for making HTTP requests to external resources.

Can be used to fetch data from APIs or other websites.

6. Mojo::Template:

A powerful template engine for generating HTML and other content.

Uses a simple syntax for embedding Perl code within templates.

Example:

Perl

```perl
use Mojo::Application;

my $app = Mojo::Application->new;

$app->get('/hello/:name', sub {
    my $self = shift;
                $self->res->body("Hello,      "    .
$self->req->param('name'));
});

$app->start;
```

This simple example demonstrates how to create a basic Mojo application that handles a GET request and responds with a greeting message.

1.2 Advanced Memory Management Techniques in Mojo

Mojo provides several tools and techniques for efficient memory management, which is crucial for building scalable and performant applications. Here are some advanced memory management techniques:

1. Weak References

Purpose: Create references to objects that don't prevent them from being garbage collected.

Usage: Use `Mojo::Util::weakref` to create a weak reference to an object. If the object is no longer referenced by any other objects, it can be garbage collected.

Perl

```perl
use Mojo::Util;

my $data = { name => 'John', age => 30 };
my $weak_ref = weakref($data);

# ... do something with the data

if ($weak_ref->is_dead) {
    print "Data has been garbage collected\n";
}
```

2. Reference Counting

Purpose: Track the number of references to an object.

Usage: Use `Mojo::Util::refcount` to get the reference count of an object.

Perl

```perl
use Mojo::Util;

my $data = { name => 'John', age => 30 };
my $ref_count = Mojo::Util::refcount($data);
print "Reference count: $ref_count\n";
```

3. Manual Memory Management

Purpose: In rare cases, you may need to manually manage memory.

Usage: Use `Mojo::Util::malloc` and `Mojo::Util::free` to allocate and free memory.

Perl

```perl
use Mojo::Util;

my $ptr = Mojo::Util::malloc(100);
# ... use the memory
Mojo::Util::free($ptr);
```

4. Memory Pooling

Purpose: Improve performance by pre-allocating memory and reusing it.

Usage: Create custom memory pools using `Mojo::Util::malloc` and `Mojo::Util::free`.

5. Garbage Collection Optimization

Purpose: Optimize the garbage collector's behavior.

Usage: Adjust the garbage collector's settings using environment variables or configuration options.

Note: While Mojo's garbage collector is generally efficient, understanding these advanced techniques can help you optimize memory usage in specific scenarios.

1.3 Customizing Mojo's Behavior

Mojo is a highly customizable framework, allowing you to tailor its behavior to your specific needs. Here are some ways to customize Mojo:

1. Creating Custom Middleware

Purpose: Add custom logic to the request/response pipeline.

Usage: Create a new `Mojo::Middleware` object and define a callback function that will be executed for each request.

Perl

```
use Mojo::Middleware;
```

```perl
my $middleware = Mojo::Middleware->new(
    sub {
        my $self = shift;
            # Do something before the request is
handled
        $self->next;
            # Do something after the request is
handled
    }
);

$app->middleware($middleware);
```

2. Modifying Built-in Components

Purpose: Customize the behavior of built-in components like `Mojo::Router` or `Mojo::Template`.

Usage: Create subclasses of these components and override their methods.

Perl

```perl
use Mojo::Router;

my $router = Mojo::Router->new;

$router->get('/hello/:name', sub {
    my $self = shift;
    # Custom logic here
    $self->next;
});
```

3. Extending Mojo's Core Classes

Purpose: Create new classes based on Mojo's core classes.

Usage: Create subclasses of `Mojo::Application`, `Mojo::Request`, or `Mojo::Response` and add custom methods or behavior.

Perl

```perl
use Mojo::Application;

my $app = Mojo::Application->new;

$app->add_hook('before_start', sub {
    # Custom logic before the application starts
});
```

4. Using Configuration Options

Purpose: Configure Mojo's behavior using environment variables or configuration files.

Usage: Set configuration options using `Mojo::Config`.

Perl

```perl
use Mojo::Config;

Mojo::Config->load('config.yml');

my $app = Mojo::Application->new;
```

5. Creating Custom Plugins

Purpose: Extend Mojo's functionality with reusable modules.

Usage: Create a new plugin module and register it with Mojo.

Perl

```perl
use Mojo::Plugin;

my $plugin = Mojo::Plugin->new(
    name       => 'MyPlugin',
    version    => '0.1',
    requires   => ['Mojo'],
    init       => sub {
        # Initialize the plugin
    }
);


Mojo->plugin($plugin);
```

By using these techniques, you can customize Mojo to fit your specific needs and build powerful and flexible web applications.

Chapter 2: Mastering Mojo's Asynchronous Programming Model

2.1 Deep Dive into Mojo's Event Loop

Mojo's event loop is a fundamental component that drives the asynchronous nature of the framework. It allows Mojo to handle multiple concurrent requests efficiently without blocking the main thread.

Understanding the Event Loop

Non-blocking I/O: Mojo's event loop uses non-blocking I/O operations, which means that it doesn't wait for a complete operation to finish before proceeding to the next one.

Event-driven architecture: The event loop listens for events (e.g., network connections, file I/O, timers) and dispatches them to appropriate handlers.

Single-threaded: Mojo's event loop is typically single-threaded, meaning it runs in a single thread of execution.

Key Concepts

Event handlers: Functions that are executed when specific events occur.

Event queues: Data structures that store events waiting to be processed.

Event loop: The main loop that continuously checks for events and dispatches them to their corresponding handlers.

How Mojo's Event Loop Works

Initialization: When a Mojo application starts, the event loop is initialized.

Event registration: Event handlers are registered with the event loop, specifying the types of events they are interested in.

Event polling: The event loop continuously polls for events using underlying operating system functions.

Event dispatching: When an event occurs, it is added to the appropriate event queue. The event loop then dispatches the event to its corresponding handler.

Handler execution: The handler function is executed, performing the necessary actions to process the event.

Loop continuation: After the handler finishes, the event loop returns to polling for more events.

Benefits of Mojo's Event Loop

High performance: Asynchronous I/O and a single-threaded event loop can lead to significant performance improvements.

Scalability: Mojo can handle a large number of concurrent connections efficiently.

Non-blocking operations: Mojo's event loop allows for non-blocking operations, preventing the application from being blocked by long-running tasks.

Advanced Techniques

Custom event loops: In some cases, you may need to create custom event loops for specific use cases.

Asynchronous programming patterns: Mojo provides patterns like promises and callbacks for writing asynchronous code effectively.

Event loop optimization: You can optimize the event loop's performance by tuning certain parameters or avoiding blocking operations.

By understanding how Mojo's event loop works, you can write more efficient and scalable applications.

2.2 Building Scalable Applications with Mojo's Async Features

Mojo's asynchronous programming model is a powerful tool for building scalable and high-performance applications. By leveraging Mojo's asynchronous features, you can handle a large number of concurrent requests efficiently without blocking the main thread.

Key Async Features

Promises: A pattern for representing the eventual result of an asynchronous operation.

Callbacks: Functions that are called when an asynchronous operation completes.

Non-blocking I/O: Mojo's event loop uses non-blocking I/O operations, allowing multiple requests to be processed concurrently.

Building Scalable Applications

Use Promises: Promises provide a clean and concise way to handle asynchronous operations. When you call an asynchronous function, it returns a promise that represents the eventual result. You can then chain promises together to create complex asynchronous workflows.

Perl

```perl
use Mojo::Promise;


my $promise = Mojo::Promise->new;


# Simulate an asynchronous operation

Mojo::Util->sleep(1);


$promise->resolve('Hello, world!');


$promise->then(sub {

    my $result = shift;

    print "Result: $result\n";

});
```

Leverage Non-blocking I/O: Mojo's event loop uses non-blocking I/O operations, which means that it doesn't wait for a complete operation to finish before proceeding to the next one. This allows Mojo to handle many concurrent requests efficiently.

Perl

```perl
use Mojo::UserAgent;


my $ua = Mojo::UserAgent->new;


$ua->get('https://example.com')->then(sub {

    my $res = shift;

    print $res->body;

});
```

Avoid Blocking Operations: Try to avoid blocking operations within your asynchronous code. Blocking operations can prevent the event loop from processing other requests.

Optimize Database Access: Use asynchronous database drivers to avoid blocking the event loop when performing database operations.

Use Connection Pools: Create connection pools for database connections or network connections to reduce the overhead of establishing new connections.

Monitor Performance: Use profiling tools to identify performance bottlenecks and optimize your application accordingly.

By following these guidelines, you can build scalable and high-performance applications using Mojo's asynchronous features.

2.3 Advanced Techniques for Handling Asynchronous I/O in Mojo

Mojo provides several advanced techniques for handling asynchronous I/O operations, allowing you to build highly efficient and scalable applications. Here are some key techniques:

1. Using Mojo::Promise

Chaining promises: Use `then` and `catch` methods to chain promises together, creating complex asynchronous workflows.

Error handling: Use `catch` to handle errors that may occur during asynchronous operations.

Perl

```perl
use Mojo::Promise;



my $promise = Mojo::Promise->new;



$promise->resolve(42);



$promise

    ->then(sub {
```

```perl
    my $result = shift;

    return $result * 2;

})

->then(sub {

    my $result = shift;

    print "Result: $result\n";

})

->catch(sub {

    my $error = shift;

    print "Error: $error\n";

});
```

2. Using Mojo::Async

Creating asynchronous tasks: Use `Mojo::Async->start` to create asynchronous tasks that can be run concurrently.

Waiting for tasks to complete: Use `Mojo::Async->wait` to wait for a group of tasks to complete.

Perl

```perl
use Mojo::Async;


my $task1 = Mojo::Async->start(sub {
```

```perl
    # Asynchronous operation 1

    return 10;

});


my $task2 = Mojo::Async->start(sub {

    # Asynchronous operation 2

    return 20;

});


Mojo::Async->wait($task1, $task2)->then(sub {

    my ($result1, $result2) = @_;

    print "Results: $result1, $result2\n";

});
```

3. Using Mojo::Reactor

Customizing the event loop: Use `Mojo::Reactor` to create custom event loops or modify the default event loop.

Perl

```perl
use Mojo::Reactor;
```

```
my $reactor = Mojo::Reactor->new;


# ... configure the reactor


$reactor->run;
```

4. Optimizing Network I/O

Using TCP keep-alive: Keep connections alive to avoid unnecessary reconnections.

Adjusting socket options: Set socket options to optimize performance for specific network environments.

Using connection pooling: Create connection pools to reuse connections and reduce overhead.

5. Handling Timeouts

Setting timeouts: Use `Mojo::UserAgent`'s `timeout` option to set timeouts for HTTP requests.

Handling timeouts: Use `Mojo::Promise`'s `timeout` method to handle timeouts for asynchronous operations.

By mastering these advanced techniques, you can write more efficient and scalable asynchronous applications in Mojo.

Chapter 3: Leveraging Mojo's Networking Capabilities

3.1 Building High-Performance HTTP Servers and Clients in Mojo

Mojo provides powerful tools for building high-performance HTTP servers and clients. By leveraging Mojo's asynchronous features and efficient networking capabilities, you can create scalable and responsive web applications.

Building High-Performance HTTP Servers

Use Mojo::Application: The `Mojo::Application` class provides a simple and efficient way to create HTTP servers.

Optimize routing: Use efficient routing algorithms to match incoming requests to the appropriate handlers.

Handle asynchronous requests: Use Mojo's asynchronous features to handle multiple requests concurrently without blocking the main thread.

Cache static assets: Cache static assets like CSS, JavaScript, and images to improve performance.

Compress responses: Use gzip compression to reduce the size of responses and improve transfer speeds.

Optimize database access: Use asynchronous database drivers and connection pooling to avoid blocking the event loop.

Example:

Perl

```perl
use Mojo::Application;


my $app = Mojo::Application->new;


$app->get('/', sub {

    my $self = shift;

    $self->res->body('Hello, world!');

});


$app->start;
```

Building High-Performance HTTP Clients

Use Mojo::UserAgent: The `Mojo::UserAgent` class provides a flexible and efficient way to make HTTP requests.

Handle asynchronous requests: Use Mojo's asynchronous features to make non-blocking HTTP requests.

Optimize network I/O: Use techniques like keep-alive connections and connection pooling to improve network performance.

Handle timeouts: Set timeouts for HTTP requests to avoid blocking the application.

Example:

Perl

```perl
use Mojo::UserAgent;


my $ua = Mojo::UserAgent->new;


$ua->get('https://example.com')->then(sub {

    my $res = shift;

    print $res->body;

});
```

Additional Tips

Use profiling tools: Identify performance bottlenecks using profiling tools like `Mojo::Profiler`.

Optimize memory usage: Avoid creating unnecessary objects and use memory management techniques like weak references.

Consider using a load balancer: Distribute traffic across multiple servers to improve scalability.

By following these guidelines, you can build high-performance HTTP servers and clients in Mojo that can handle large volumes of traffic efficiently.

3.2 Implementing Custom Network Protocols in Mojo

Mojo provides a powerful framework for building custom network protocols. By leveraging Mojo's asynchronous features and networking capabilities, you can create custom protocols tailored to your specific needs.

Key Steps

Define the Protocol: Clearly define the protocol's syntax, semantics, and message formats.

Implement the Protocol Parser: Create a parser to decode incoming messages and extract the relevant data.

Implement the Protocol Encoder: Create an encoder to encode outgoing messages into the protocol's format.

Create a Network Handler: Create a network handler that will handle incoming connections and process messages.

Integrate with Mojo: Integrate your custom protocol with Mojo's event loop and networking components.

Example: A Simple Custom Protocol

Perl

```perl
use Mojo::TCP;


my $protocol = {

    # Protocol definition
```

```perl
};


my $handler = Mojo::TCP->new(

    listen => 'localhost:8080',

    on_accept => sub {

        my $self = shift;

        $self->peer->on_read(sub {

            my $self = shift;

            my $data = $self->data;

            # Parse the incoming data

            my $message = parse_message($data);

            # Process the message

                            my    $response    =
create_response($message);

            $self->peer->send($response);

        });

    }

);


$handler->start;
```

Advanced Techniques

Using Mojo::Protocol: The `Mojo::Protocol` class provides a convenient way to define and implement custom protocols.

Leveraging Mojo's networking components: Use `Mojo::TCP`, `Mojo::UDP`, and other networking components to handle different types of connections.

Optimizing performance: Use techniques like buffering, pipelining, and compression to improve performance.

Handling errors and exceptions: Implement error handling mechanisms to gracefully handle unexpected situations.

Additional Considerations

Security: Ensure that your custom protocol is secure and resistant to attacks.

Compatibility: Consider compatibility with existing protocols or standards.

Testing: Thoroughly test your custom protocol to ensure it works as expected.

By following these steps and leveraging Mojo's powerful features, you can create custom network protocols that meet your specific requirements.

3.3 Advanced TCP/IP Socket Programming in Mojo

Mojo provides a powerful and flexible API for working with TCP/IP sockets. By leveraging Mojo's asynchronous features and networking capabilities, you can build high-performance network applications.

Key Concepts

Mojo::TCP: The primary class for creating TCP sockets.

Non-blocking I/O: Mojo's TCP sockets use non-blocking I/O, allowing multiple connections to be handled concurrently without blocking the main thread.

Asynchronous operations: Use Mojo's asynchronous features to perform operations like reading and writing data without blocking.

Common Use Cases

Creating TCP servers: Build servers that listen for incoming connections and handle client requests.

Creating TCP clients: Connect to remote servers and send/receive data.

Implementing custom network protocols: Build custom network protocols on top of TCP.

Advanced Techniques

Socket options: Set socket options to customize the behavior of TCP connections, such as timeouts, keep-alive, and buffer sizes.

Asynchronous I/O: Use `on_read`, `on_write`, and other event handlers to handle asynchronous I/O operations.

Error handling: Implement error handling mechanisms to gracefully handle errors and exceptions.

Performance optimization: Use techniques like connection pooling, pipelining, and compression to improve performance.

Example: Creating a Simple TCP Server

Perl

```perl
use Mojo::TCP;

my $server = Mojo::TCP->new(
    listen => 'localhost:8080',
    on_accept => sub {
        my $self = shift;
        $self->peer->on_read(sub {
            my $self = shift;
            my $data = $self->data;
            print "Received: $data\n";
            $self->peer->send("Hello, world!\n");
        });
    }
);

$server->start;
```

Additional Considerations

Security: Implement security measures to protect against attacks like denial-of-service (DoS) and man-in-the-middle (MITM).

Scalability: Consider using techniques like connection pooling and load balancing to improve scalability.

Compatibility: Ensure compatibility with different operating systems and network environments.

By mastering advanced TCP/IP socket programming in Mojo, you can build powerful and efficient network applications.

Chapter 4: Diving into Mojo's Template Engine

4.1 Advanced Template Syntax and Features in Mojo::Template

Mojo::Template provides a powerful and flexible template engine for generating HTML and other content. It offers advanced syntax features and customization options to help you create dynamic and maintainable templates.

Advanced Syntax Features

Conditional rendering: Use `if`, `elsif`, and `else` blocks to conditionally render content based on conditions.

Loops: Use `foreach` loops to iterate over arrays and hashes.

Custom filters: Create custom filters to modify or format data before rendering.

Template inheritance: Use template inheritance to create reusable template components.

Custom tags: Define custom tags to encapsulate complex logic within templates.

Example: Using Conditional Rendering and Loops

Perl

```perl
use Mojo::Template;

my $template = Mojo::Template->new;
```

```perl
$template->render(
    template => 'my_template.html.ep',
    data     => {
        items => [
            { name => 'Item 1', price => 10 },
            { name => 'Item 2', price => 20 },
        ]
    }
);
```

Customizing Mojo::Template

Setting options: Use `options` to set various options for the template engine, such as `auto_escape` and `strict`.

Creating custom filters: Create custom filters using Perl code to modify or format data.

Defining custom tags: Define custom tags using Perl code to encapsulate complex logic within templates.

Example: Creating a Custom Filter

Perl

```perl
use Mojo::Template;

my $template = Mojo::Template->new;
$template->filter(
    capitalize => sub {
        my $text = shift;
        return ucfirst($text);
    }
```

```
) ;
```

Best Practices

Keep templates clean and maintainable: Use clear and concise syntax, and avoid complex logic within templates.

Use template inheritance: Break down large templates into smaller, reusable components.

Test templates thoroughly: Ensure that your templates render correctly with different data inputs.

By mastering advanced template syntax and features in Mojo::Template, you can create dynamic and efficient web applications.

4.2 Customizing Mojo's Template Engine

Mojo's template engine is highly customizable, allowing you to tailor its behavior to your specific needs. Here are some ways to customize Mojo::Template:

1. Setting Options

auto_escape: Enable or disable automatic HTML escaping.

strict: Enable strict mode for template validation.

cache: Enable or disable template caching.

trim: Trim whitespace from the beginning and end of template output.

Perl

```
use Mojo::Template;

my $template = Mojo::Template->new(
    auto_escape => 1,
    strict      => 1,
    cache       => 1,
);
```

2. Creating Custom Filters

Define custom functions: Create Perl functions that will be used to transform data within templates.

Register filters: Register the custom functions with Mojo::Template.

Perl

```
use Mojo::Template;

my $template = Mojo::Template->new;
$template->filter(
    capitalize => sub {
        my $text = shift;
        return ucfirst($text);
    }
);
```

3. Defining Custom Tags

Create custom tags: Define custom tags using Perl code.

Register tags: Register the custom tags with Mojo::Template.

Perl

```perl
use Mojo::Template;

my $template = Mojo::Template->new;
$template->tag(
    'my_tag' => sub {
        my $self = shift;
        # Custom logic here
        return 'Hello, world!';
    }
);
```

4. Extending Mojo::Template

Create subclasses: Create subclasses of `Mojo::Template` to add custom functionality.

Override methods: Override methods like `render` or `parse` to modify the template engine's behavior.

Perl

```perl
use Mojo::Template;

my $my_template = Mojo::Template->new;
$my_template->override(
    render => sub {
        my $self = shift;
        # Custom rendering logic here
        return $self->SUPER::render(@_);
    }
```

```
);
```

5. Using Template Inheritance

Create base templates: Create base templates that define common layout and structure.

Extend base templates: Extend base templates in child templates to add specific content.

By using these techniques, you can customize Mojo::Template to fit your specific needs and create more flexible and maintainable templates.

4.3 Building Dynamic Web Applications with Mojo

Mojo provides a powerful framework for building dynamic web applications. By combining its template engine, routing system, and asynchronous capabilities, you can create interactive and responsive web experiences.

Key Components

Mojo::Application: The foundation of a Mojo web application.

Mojo::Router: Defines routes and associates them with handlers.

Mojo::Template: Generates HTML content using templates.

Mojo::Request: Represents incoming HTTP requests.

Mojo::Response: Represents outgoing HTTP responses.

Building Dynamic Web Applications

Create a Mojo application: Instantiate a `Mojo::Application` object.

Define routes: Use `Mojo::Router` to define routes and associate them with handlers.

Render templates: Use `Mojo::Template` to render HTML content based on data.

Handle form submissions: Use `Mojo::Request` to access form data and process submissions.

Use asynchronous features: Leverage Mojo's asynchronous capabilities to handle multiple requests concurrently and avoid blocking the main thread.

Example: A Simple Dynamic Web Application

Perl

```perl
use Mojo::Application;
use Mojo::Template;

my $app = Mojo::Application->new;
my $template = Mojo::Template->new;

$app->get('/', sub {
    my $self = shift;
    my $data = {
        message => 'Hello, world!'
    };
    $self->res->body($template->render(
        template => 'index.html.ep',
        data     => $data
    ));
```

```
});

$app->start;
```

Additional Features

Session management: Use Mojo's built-in session management features to store user data across requests.

Database integration: Integrate with databases using Mojo's database drivers.

WebSockets: Use WebSockets for real-time communication between the client and server.

Authentication and authorization: Implement authentication and authorization mechanisms to protect sensitive resources.

By combining these components and features, you can create dynamic and interactive web applications using Mojo.

Chapter 5: Exploring Mojo's Database Integration

5.1 Integrating with Popular Databases in Mojo

Mojo provides a robust framework for integrating with popular databases like PostgreSQL and MySQL. By leveraging Mojo's asynchronous features and database drivers, you can easily build data-driven web applications.

Key Components

Mojo::DB: The base class for database drivers in Mojo.

Mojo::DB::Pg: The PostgreSQL database driver.

Mojo::DB::MySQL: The MySQL database driver.

Connecting to a Database

Perl

```perl
use Mojo::DB::Pg;

my $db = Mojo::DB::Pg->new(
                                  dsn          =>
'dbi:Pg:dbname=my_database;host=localhost;port=54
32',
    user => 'my_user',
    pass => 'my_password'
);
```

Executing Queries

Perl

```perl
$db->query('SELECT * FROM my_table')
    ->then(sub {
        my $results = shift;
        # Process the results
    });
```

Using Prepared Statements

Perl

```perl
my $sth = $db->prepare('SELECT * FROM my_table
WHERE name = ?');

$sth->execute('John');

while (my $row = $sth->fetchrow_hashref) {
    # Process the row
}
```

Asynchronous Operations

Mojo's database drivers are asynchronous, allowing you to perform database operations without blocking the main thread. This is especially important for web applications that need to handle multiple concurrent requests.

Additional Features

Transaction support: Use transactions to ensure data consistency.

Custom data types: Define custom data types for specific database requirements.

Query builders: Use query builders to construct complex SQL queries more easily.

Example: A Simple CRUD Operation

Perl

```perl
use Mojo::DB::Pg;

my $db = Mojo::DB::Pg->new(
    # Database connection details
);

# Create a new user
$db->query('INSERT  INTO  users  (name,  email)
VALUES (?, ?)', 'John Doe', 'john@example.com');

# Retrieve all users
$db->query('SELECT * FROM users')
    ->then(sub {
        my $results = shift;
        # Process the results
    });

# Update a user
$db->query('UPDATE users SET email = ? WHERE id =
?', 'new_email@example.com', 1);
```

```
# Delete a user
$db->query('DELETE FROM users WHERE id = ?', 2);
```

By leveraging Mojo's database integration features, you can efficiently interact with popular databases and build data-driven web applications.

5.2 Advanced Database Query Techniques in Mojo

Mojo's database drivers provide a powerful and flexible API for executing database queries. By mastering advanced query techniques, you can optimize your database interactions and improve the performance of your applications.

1. Indexing

Purpose: Improve query performance by creating indexes on frequently queried columns.

Techniques: Use CREATE INDEX statements to create indexes. Consider creating composite indexes for multiple columns.

SQL

```
CREATE INDEX idx_users_name ON users (name);
```

2. Query Optimization

Explain plans: Use `EXPLAIN` to analyze query execution plans and identify performance bottlenecks.

Query rewriting: Rewrite queries to improve performance, such as using JOINs instead of subqueries.

Query caching: Use query caching mechanisms provided by your database to avoid re-executing the same query multiple times.

3. Pagination

Purpose: Handle large result sets efficiently by retrieving data in smaller chunks.

Techniques: Use `LIMIT` and `OFFSET` clauses to paginate results.

SQL

```
SELECT * FROM my_table LIMIT 10 OFFSET 20;
```

4. Stored Procedures

Purpose: Encapsulate complex database logic and improve performance.

Techniques: Create stored procedures using your database's specific syntax.

SQL

```
CREATE    PROCEDURE    get_users_by_name(IN    name
VARCHAR(50))
BEGIN
```

```
    SELECT * FROM users WHERE name = name;
END;
```

5. Full-Text Search

Purpose: Efficiently search for text within large datasets.

Techniques: Use full-text search features provided by your database, such as `FTS` in PostgreSQL or `FULLTEXT` in MySQL.

6. Database-Specific Features

Explore database-specific features: Different databases may have unique features and optimizations that can improve query performance.

Example: Using Indexes and Pagination

Perl

```perl
use Mojo::DB::Pg;

my $db = Mojo::DB::Pg->new(
    # Database connection details
);

# Create an index on the 'name' column
$db->query('CREATE INDEX idx_users_name ON users
(name)');

# Retrieve paginated results
```

```
$db->query('SELECT * FROM users WHERE name LIKE ?
ORDER BY id LIMIT 10 OFFSET ?', '%John%', 20)
    ->then(sub {
        my $results = shift;
        # Process the results
    });
```

By mastering these advanced database query techniques, you can optimize your database interactions and improve the performance of your Mojo applications.

5.3 Building Data-Driven Applications with Mojo

Mojo provides a robust framework for building data-driven applications. By integrating with databases and leveraging Mojo's asynchronous features, you can create dynamic and interactive web applications that rely on data.

Key Components

Mojo::DB: The base class for database drivers in Mojo.

Mojo::Template: For rendering HTML templates.

Mojo::Router: For defining routes and handling requests.

Steps to Build a Data-Driven Application

Connect to a database: Use Mojo's database drivers (e.g., `Mojo::DB::Pg`, `Mojo::DB::MySQL`) to connect to your chosen database.

Retrieve data: Query the database to fetch the necessary data.

Pass data to templates: Pass the retrieved data to templates for rendering.

Render templates: Use Mojo's template engine to generate HTML content based on the data.

Handle user interactions: Handle user interactions, such as form submissions or AJAX requests, to update the data and re-render the page.

Example: A Simple Blog Application

Perl

```perl
use Mojo::Application;
use Mojo::Template;
use Mojo::DB::Pg;

my $app = Mojo::Application->new;
my $template = Mojo::Template->new;
my $db = Mojo::DB::Pg->new(
    # Database connection details
);

$app->get('/', sub {
    my $self = shift;
    $db->query('SELECT * FROM posts')
        ->then(sub {
            my $posts = shift;
            $self->res->body($template->render(
                template => 'index.html.ep',
                data     => { posts => $posts }
            ));
        });
});
```

```
$app->start;
```

Additional Considerations

Data validation: Validate user input to ensure data integrity.

Security: Implement security measures to protect against SQL injection and other attacks.

Caching: Use caching techniques to improve performance for frequently accessed data.

Asynchronous operations: Leverage Mojo's asynchronous features to handle database operations efficiently.

Error handling: Implement proper error handling to provide informative feedback to users.

By following these steps and incorporating best practices, you can build robust and data-driven web applications using Mojo.

Chapter 6: Building RESTful APIs with Mojo

6.1 Designing and Implementing RESTful APIs with Mojo

Mojo provides a powerful framework for building RESTful APIs. By adhering to REST principles and leveraging Mojo's features, you can create well-structured and scalable APIs.

REST Principles

Resource-based: APIs should be designed around resources, such as users, products, or posts.

Stateless: Each request should be treated independently, without relying on previous requests.

Cacheable: Responses should be cacheable where appropriate to improve performance.

Client-server: The client and server should be separated, with the client responsible for managing the user interface and the server responsible for handling data and business logic.

Layered system: APIs can be layered to support different levels of abstraction.

Uniform interface: Use a uniform interface for interacting with resources, such as HTTP methods (GET, POST, PUT, DELETE) and URIs.

Implementing RESTful APIs in Mojo

Define resources: Identify the resources that your API will expose.

Design URIs: Create URIs that represent resources using nouns.

Use HTTP methods: Use appropriate HTTP methods to perform different actions on resources:

- **GET:** Retrieve a resource.
- **POST:** Create a new resource.
- **PUT:** Update an existing resource.
- **DELETE:** Delete a resource.

Return appropriate status codes: Use HTTP status codes to indicate the success or failure of requests.

Use JSON as the data format: JSON is a popular format for representing data in REST APIs.

Leverage Mojo's features: Use Mojo's routing system, template engine, and database integration to build your API.

Example: A Simple RESTful API

Perl

```perl
use Mojo::Application;

my $app = Mojo::Application->new;

$app->get('/users/:id', sub {
    my $self = shift;
    my $id = $self->req->param('id');
    # Retrieve user data from the database
    my $user = get_user($id);
    $self->res->json($user);
```

```
});

$app->post('/users', sub {
    my $self = shift;
    my $data = $self->req->json;
    # Create a new user in the database
    my $new_user = create_user($data);
    $self->res->json($new_user);
});

$app->start;
```

Additional Considerations

Versioning: Consider versioning your API to support backward compatibility.

Authentication and authorization: Implement authentication and authorization mechanisms to protect sensitive resources.

Error handling: Provide informative error messages and appropriate status codes.

Documentation: Document your API to help developers understand how to use it.

By following these guidelines, you can create well-structured and scalable RESTful APIs using Mojo.

6.2 Handling API Authentication and Authorization in Mojo

When building RESTful APIs, it's essential to implement robust authentication and authorization mechanisms to protect sensitive resources. Mojo provides several options for handling API authentication and authorization.

1. API Keys

Simple: Assign unique API keys to clients.

Validation: Validate API keys on each request.

Security: Consider using HTTPS to protect API keys in transit.

Example:

Perl

```perl
use Mojo::Application;

my $app = Mojo::Application->new;

$app->get('/protected', sub {
    my $self = shift;
                        my      $api_key      =
$self->req->headers->get('Authorization');
    unless (validate_api_key($api_key)) {
        $self->res->status(401);
        return;
    }
    # ... protected resource logic
});

$app->start;
```

2. OAuth 2.0

Standard: Adheres to the OAuth 2.0 standard for authorization.

Flexibility: Supports various authorization flows (authorization code, implicit, client credentials, password).

Complexity: Requires more complex implementation.

Example:

Perl

```perl
use Mojo::Application;
use Mojo::OAuth2;

my $app = Mojo::Application->new;

my $oauth = Mojo::OAuth2->new(
    client_id      => 'your_client_id',
    client_secret => 'your_client_secret',
                        authorize_url         =>
'https://example.com/authorize',
    token_url       => 'https://example.com/token'
);

$app->get('/protected', sub {
    my $self = shift;
                    my      $access_token      =
$self->req->headers->get('Authorization');
                                            unless
($oauth->validate_token($access_token)) {
        $self->res->status(401);
        return;
    }
    # ... protected resource logic
});
```

```perl
$app->start;
```

3. JWT (JSON Web Tokens)

Lightweight: Compact and easy to use.

Secure: Can be signed and encrypted for added security.

Customizable: Can be customized to include claims about the user.

Example:

Perl

```perl
use Mojo::Application;
use Mojo::JWT;

my $app = Mojo::Application->new;

my $jwt = Mojo::JWT->new(
    secret => 'your_secret'
);

$app->get('/protected', sub {
    my $self = shift;
                my      $authorization_header      =
$self->req->headers->get('Authorization');
        unless ($authorization_header =~ /^Bearer
(.+)$/) {
        $self->res->status(401);
        return;
    }
    my $token = $1;
    unless ($jwt->validate($token)) {
```

```perl
        $self->res->status(401);
        return;
    }
    # ... protected resource logic
});

$app->start;
```

Additional Considerations

Rate limiting: Implement rate limiting to prevent abuse.

IP address restrictions: Restrict access based on IP address.

Monitoring and logging: Monitor API usage and log access attempts.

Security best practices: Follow security best practices, such as using HTTPS and avoiding hardcoding credentials.

By carefully considering your API's requirements and choosing the appropriate authentication and authorization mechanism, you can effectively protect your API from unauthorized access.

6.3 Building Scalable and Efficient APIs with Mojo

When designing and implementing RESTful APIs, scalability and efficiency are crucial factors to consider. By following these best practices, you can create APIs that can handle increasing loads and perform optimally.

1. Caching

Leverage browser caching: Enable caching for static assets (CSS, JavaScript, images) to reduce server load.

Implement server-side caching: Cache frequently accessed data to avoid redundant database queries.

Use conditional requests: Use HTTP headers like `If-Modified-Since` and `If-None-Match` to avoid sending unnecessary data.

2. Asynchronous Operations

Use asynchronous I/O: Mojo's asynchronous features allow you to handle multiple requests concurrently without blocking the main thread.

Optimize database access: Use asynchronous database drivers and connection pooling to improve performance.

3. API Rate Limiting

Prevent abuse: Limit the number of requests a client can make within a certain time period.

Implement rate limiting: Use tools like `Mojo::RateLimit` or custom implementations.

4. Efficient Data Formats

Use JSON: JSON is a lightweight and efficient data format.

Consider alternatives: For large datasets, consider using more efficient formats like Protocol Buffers or MessagePack.

5. Optimize Network I/O

Use keep-alive connections: Keep connections open between requests to reduce overhead.

Compress responses: Use compression techniques like gzip to reduce data transfer size.

6. Database Optimization

Indexing: Create indexes on frequently queried columns to improve query performance.

Query optimization: Use techniques like query rewriting and explain plans to identify and address performance bottlenecks.

Database sharding: Distribute data across multiple databases to improve scalability.

7. Server Configuration

Tune server settings: Optimize your server's configuration for performance, such as increasing worker processes or adjusting memory limits.

Use a load balancer: Distribute traffic across multiple servers to improve scalability.

8. Monitoring and Profiling

Monitor performance: Use tools to monitor your API's performance and identify bottlenecks.

Profile code: Use profiling tools to analyze code execution and identify performance hotspots.

By following these guidelines, you can build scalable and efficient APIs that can handle increasing loads and provide a great user experience.

Chapter 7: Advanced Mojo Web Development

7.1 Building Single-Page Applications (SPAs) with Mojo

Mojo can be used to build Single-Page Applications (SPAs), which provide a more interactive and responsive user experience compared to traditional multi-page applications.

Key Components

Mojo::Application: The foundation of a Mojo web application.

Mojo::Template: For rendering HTML content.

JavaScript framework: A JavaScript framework like React, Vue, or Angular to handle client-side logic.

API endpoints: RESTful APIs to fetch and update data from the server.

Steps to Build a SPA

Create a Mojo application: Instantiate a `Mojo::Application` object.

Define routes: Use `Mojo::Router` to define routes and associate them with handlers.

Render the initial HTML: Render the initial HTML structure of the SPA.

Serve static assets: Serve static assets like JavaScript, CSS, and images.

Create API endpoints: Define RESTful APIs to fetch and update data from the server.

Use a JavaScript framework: Use a JavaScript framework to handle client-side logic, including rendering dynamic content, handling user interactions, and making AJAX requests to the API.

Example: A Simple SPA with React

Perl

```perl
use Mojo::Application;
use Mojo::Template;

my $app = Mojo::Application->new;
my $template = Mojo::Template->new;

$app->get('/', sub {
    my $self = shift;
    $self->res->body($template->render(
        template => 'index.html.ep'
    ));
});

$app->static('/static', { root => 'public' });

$app->start;
```

index.html.ep:

HTML

```html
<!DOCTYPE html>
<html>
<head>
```

```html
    <title>My SPA</title>
</head>
<body>
    <div id="app"></div>

                                                    <script
src="https://unpkg.com/react@18.2.0/umd/react.dev
elopment.js"></script>

                                                    <script
src="https://unpkg.com/react-dom@18.2.0/umd/react
-dom.development.js"></script>
    <script    src="static/main.js"></script>
</body>
</html>
```

main.js:

JavaScript

```javascript
import React from 'react';
import ReactDOM from 'react-dom/client';

const App = () => {
    // ... React component logic
};

const                          root                          =
ReactDOM.createRoot(document.getElementById('app'
));
root.render(<App />);
```

Additional Considerations

State management: Use a state management library like Redux or Zustand to manage application state.

Routing: Use a routing library like React Router or Vue Router to handle navigation within the SPA.

Data fetching: Use libraries like Axios or fetch to make AJAX requests to the API.

Performance optimization: Optimize your SPA for performance by using techniques like code splitting, lazy loading, and caching.

By following these steps and leveraging the power of Mojo and a JavaScript framework, you can build interactive and responsive SPAs.

7.2 Implementing WebSockets for Real-Time Communication in Mojo

WebSockets provide a full-duplex communication channel between a client and a server, allowing for real-time updates and two-way communication. Mojo offers built-in support for WebSockets, making it easy to implement real-time features in your web applications.

Key Components

Mojo::WebSocket: Represents a WebSocket connection.

Mojo::WebSocket::Server: Creates a WebSocket server.

Mojo::WebSocket::Client: Creates a WebSocket client.

Creating a WebSocket Server

Perl

```perl
use Mojo::WebSocket::Server;

my $server = Mojo::WebSocket::Server->new(
    listen => 'localhost:8080',
    on_connect => sub {
        my $self = shift;
        $self->peer->on_message(sub {
            my $self = shift;
            my $message = $self->data;
            # Process the message
            $self->send("You sent: $message");
        });
    }
);

$server->start;
```

Creating a WebSocket Client

Perl

```perl
use Mojo::WebSocket::Client;

my $client = Mojo::WebSocket::Client->new;

$client->connect('ws://localhost:8080')->then(sub {
    my $ws = shift;
    $ws->send('Hello from the client!');
    $ws->on_message(sub {
```

```perl
    my $self = shift;
    my $message = $self->data;
    print "Received: $message\n";
  });
});
```

Key Features

Full-duplex communication: Both the client and server can send and receive messages.

Asynchronous I/O: WebSockets use asynchronous I/O, allowing for efficient handling of multiple concurrent connections.

Message-based communication: Messages are transmitted as text or binary data.

Persistent connections: WebSocket connections remain open until explicitly closed, allowing for real-time updates.

Best Practices

Error handling: Implement error handling mechanisms to gracefully handle connection errors and unexpected messages.

Security: Consider using HTTPS to secure WebSocket connections and protect against attacks.

Rate limiting: Implement rate limiting to prevent abuse.

Testing: Thoroughly test your WebSocket implementation to ensure it works as expected.

By leveraging Mojo's WebSocket support, you can easily add real-time features to your web applications, such as chat applications, real-time dashboards, and collaborative tools.

7.3 Optimizing Web Application Performance with Mojo

To ensure your Mojo web applications perform optimally, consider these optimization techniques:

1. Caching:

Static asset caching: Use a CDN or browser caching to deliver static assets like CSS, JavaScript, and images efficiently.

Server-side caching: Cache frequently accessed data to reduce database queries and improve response times.

2. Asynchronous Operations:

Leverage Mojo's asynchronous features: Use promises, callbacks, and non-blocking I/O to handle multiple requests concurrently.

Optimize database queries: Use indexes, prepared statements, and query caching to improve database performance.

3. Code Optimization:

Minimize JavaScript and CSS: Remove unnecessary code and minify files.

Optimize image sizes: Compress images and use appropriate formats (e.g., JPEG, PNG, WebP).

Reduce HTTP requests: Combine CSS and JavaScript files, and inline critical CSS.

4. Server Configuration:

Tune server settings: Optimize your web server's configuration for performance, such as increasing worker processes or adjusting memory limits.

Use a load balancer: Distribute traffic across multiple servers to improve scalability.

5. Network Optimization:

Reduce latency: Use a CDN or optimize your network infrastructure to reduce latency.

Optimize DNS resolution: Ensure your DNS is configured correctly and use DNS prefetching.

6. Profiling and Monitoring:

Use profiling tools: Identify performance bottlenecks using tools like `Mojo::Profiler`.

Monitor metrics: Track metrics like response time, CPU usage, and memory consumption.

7. Content Delivery Network (CDN):

Improve performance: Use a CDN to cache static assets and deliver them closer to users.

Reduce load on servers: Offload static content delivery to the CDN.

8. HTTP/2:

Enable HTTP/2: If your server and clients support HTTP/2, enable it to improve performance.

9. Server-Side Rendering (SSR):

Improve SEO: Render HTML on the server-side for better SEO.

Improve perceived performance: Reduce the time to first paint.

By implementing these optimization techniques, you can significantly improve the performance of your Mojo web applications, providing a better user experience and increasing your website's success.

Chapter 8: Mojo's Ecosystem: Libraries and Tools

8.1 Exploring Third-Party Mojo Libraries

Mojo's vibrant ecosystem offers a wide range of third-party libraries that can enhance your web applications. These libraries provide additional features, functionality, and convenience.

Popular Third-Party Libraries

Mojo::Session: Provides session management capabilities for storing user data across requests.

Mojo::Template::Mojolicious: A template engine based on Mojolicious's template system.

Mojo::Mail: Sends and receives emails.

Mojo::Websocket::Protocol: A framework for building custom WebSocket protocols.

Mojo::JSON::XS: A high-performance JSON parser and encoder.

Mojo::Redis: A Redis client for Mojo.

Mojo::MongoDB: A MongoDB client for Mojo.

Mojo::OAuth2: A library for implementing OAuth 2.0 authentication.

Mojo::Websocket::Protocol::Chat: A WebSocket protocol for chat applications.

Finding and Using Third-Party Libraries

Search for libraries: Use search engines or the Mojo community forums to find relevant libraries.

Install libraries: Use `cpanm` or other package managers to install libraries.

Use libraries in your code: Import the library and use its functions or classes.

Example: Using Mojo::Session for Session Management

Perl

```perl
use Mojo::Application;
use Mojo::Session;

my $app = Mojo::Application->new;

$app->middleware(Mojo::Session->new);

$app->get('/', sub {
    my $self = shift;
    my $session = $self->req->session;
                    $session->data(counter    =>
$session->data('counter') || 0);
                    $session->data(counter    =>
$session->data('counter') + 1);
            $self->res->body("Counter:     "    .
$session->data('counter'));
});

$app->start;
```

Benefits of Using Third-Party Libraries

Save development time: Re-use code written by others.

Leverage expertise: Benefit from the experience and knowledge of the library's developers.

Improve code quality: Use well-tested and maintained libraries.

Expand functionality: Access new features and capabilities.

By exploring and utilizing third-party Mojo libraries, you can enhance your web applications and streamline your development process.

8.2 Building Custom Mojo Extensions

Mojo's modular architecture allows you to create custom extensions to extend its functionality. This can be useful for adding domain-specific features or integrating with third-party systems.

Steps to Create a Custom Extension

Create a new module: Create a new Perl module in your project directory.

Define the extension: Use `Mojo::Plugin` to define your extension.

Register the extension: Register the extension with Mojo.

Implement the extension's functionality: Define methods or callbacks that will be called when the extension is used.

Example: A Custom Middleware Extension

Perl

```perl
use Mojo::Plugin;

my $plugin = Mojo::Plugin->new(
    name        => 'MyMiddleware',
    version     => '0.1',
    requires    => ['Mojo'],
    init        => sub {
        my $self = shift;
        $self->app->middleware(
            sub {
                my $self = shift;
                # Custom middleware logic
                $self->next;
            }
        );
    }
);

Mojo->plugin($plugin);
```

Customizing Extensions

Configuration options: Define configuration options for your extension.

Event handlers: Use event handlers to respond to specific events within the Mojo application.

Integration with other components: Integrate your extension with other Mojo components, such as the router or template engine.

Benefits of Creating Custom Extensions

Modularity: Break down your application into smaller, reusable components.

Reusability: Share your extensions with others or use them in multiple projects.

Customization: Tailor Mojo's functionality to your specific needs.

Additional Tips

Follow best practices: Adhere to Perl best practices for writing clean and maintainable code.

Test your extension thoroughly: Write unit tests to ensure your extension works as expected.

Document your extension: Provide clear documentation to help others understand and use your extension.

By creating custom extensions, you can tailor Mojo to your specific needs and build more powerful and flexible applications.

8.3 Leveraging Mojo's Toolchain for Development and Deployment

Mojo provides a comprehensive toolchain for developing and deploying web applications. These tools can streamline your development process and improve efficiency.

Key Tools

Mojo::Command: A command-line interface for Mojo applications.

Mojo::Server: A standalone web server for running Mojo applications.

Mojo::App::PSGI: A PSGI adapter for running Mojo applications in a PSGI environment.

Mojo::App::Starman: A high-performance PSGI server.

Mojo::App::Lite: A lightweight framework for creating simple Mojo applications.

Development Workflow

Create a new project: Use `mojo new` to create a new Mojo project.

Write your application: Develop your application using Mojo's components and APIs.

Run the application: Use `mojo run` to start your application in development mode.

Test your application: Use testing frameworks like `Test::Mojo` to test your application's functionality.

Deployment

Choose a deployment method: Decide whether to deploy your application on a standalone server, a cloud platform, or a containerized environment.

Configure your deployment environment: Set up the necessary dependencies and configurations.

Deploy your application: Use tools like `mojo deploy` or your deployment platform's specific tools to deploy your application.

Example: Using Mojo::Server for Development

Bash

```
mojo new my_app
cd my_app
mojo run
```

Additional Tools

Mojo::Debugger: A debugger for Mojo applications.

Mojo::Profiler: A profiler for analyzing application performance.

Mojo::Template::Mojolicious: A template engine based on Mojolicious's template system.

Benefits of Using Mojo's Toolchain

Simplified development: Mojo's tools make it easier to create, run, and test your applications.

Efficiency: The toolchain can help you streamline your development process and improve productivity.

Flexibility: Mojo offers a variety of tools and options to suit different deployment scenarios.

By leveraging Mojo's toolchain, you can simplify your development and deployment process and focus on building great web applications.

Chapter 9: Performance Optimization in Mojo

9.1 Profiling and Benchmarking Mojo Applications

Profiling and benchmarking are essential tools for optimizing the performance of your Mojo applications. By identifying bottlenecks and measuring performance metrics, you can make informed decisions about how to improve your application's efficiency.

Profiling Tools

Mojo::Profiler: Mojo's built-in profiler provides detailed information about code execution, memory usage, and other performance metrics.

Devel::PP: A general-purpose Perl profiler that can be used with Mojo applications.

Perl::Timer: A module for measuring the elapsed time of code execution.

Benchmarking Techniques

Measure response times: Use tools like `curl` or a browser's developer tools to measure the time it takes for your application to respond to requests.

Test under load: Simulate real-world traffic using tools like `ab` (ApacheBench) or `wrk` to assess your application's performance under load.

Profile memory usage: Use profiling tools to measure your application's memory consumption and identify memory leaks.

Analyze database queries: Use database-specific tools to analyze query performance and optimize database access.

Example: Using Mojo::Profiler

Perl

```perl
use Mojo::Application;
use Mojo::Profiler;

my $app = Mojo::Application->new;

$app->get('/', sub {
    my $self = shift;
    # ... application logic
});

Mojo::Profiler->start;
$app->start;
Mojo::Profiler->report;
```

Interpreting Profiling Results

Identify bottlenecks: Look for functions or code blocks that consume the most time or resources.

Optimize code: Rewrite code to improve performance, such as using more efficient algorithms or data structures.

Optimize database queries: Use indexes, prepared statements, and query caching to improve database performance.

Reduce memory usage: Avoid creating unnecessary objects and use memory management techniques like weak references.

Additional Tips

Use a consistent testing environment: Ensure that your benchmarking tests are conducted under consistent conditions.

Consider different workloads: Test your application under various workloads to identify performance bottlenecks in different scenarios.

Monitor performance over time: Continuously monitor your application's performance to detect any regressions.

By using profiling and benchmarking techniques, you can identify and address performance issues in your Mojo applications, ensuring that they provide a great user experience.

9.2 Optimizing Memory Usage and Garbage Collection in Mojo

Efficient memory management is crucial for building scalable and high-performance Mojo applications. By understanding how Mojo's garbage collector works and implementing best practices, you can optimize memory usage and avoid memory leaks.

Understanding Mojo's Garbage Collector

Reference counting: Mojo uses a reference counting garbage collector, which tracks the number of references to an object. When an object's reference count reaches zero, it is considered garbage and can be collected.

Cycles: The reference counting algorithm can sometimes fail to collect objects that are involved in cycles (circular references). To address this, Mojo uses a cycle collector to detect and break cycles.

Best Practices for Memory Optimization

Avoid unnecessary object creation: Minimize the creation of objects, especially short-lived objects.

Use weak references: Use `Mojo::Util::weakref` to create weak references to objects that you don't need to keep alive.

Reuse objects: Whenever possible, reuse objects instead of creating new ones.

Be mindful of closures: Closures can unintentionally capture references to objects, preventing them from being garbage collected.

Optimize data structures: Choose appropriate data structures based on your application's needs.

Profile memory usage: Use profiling tools to identify areas where memory is being used inefficiently.

Memory Leak Detection

Use profiling tools: Tools like `Mojo::Profiler` can help you identify memory leaks by tracking object allocations and deallocations.

Monitor memory usage: Monitor your application's memory consumption over time to detect any anomalies.

Check for circular references: Look for circular references that might prevent objects from being garbage collected.

Additional Tips

Use a memory profiler: A dedicated memory profiler can provide more detailed information about memory usage.

Consider using a garbage collector tuning tool: Some databases or operating systems offer tools for tuning the garbage collector's behavior.

Experiment with different memory allocation strategies: Try different memory allocation strategies to see if they improve performance.

By following these guidelines and using profiling tools, you can optimize memory usage and avoid memory leaks in your Mojo applications.

9.3 Improving Network Performance in Mojo

Network performance is a critical factor in the overall performance of web applications. By optimizing network I/O and using best practices, you can improve network performance and enhance the user experience.

Key Techniques

Use keep-alive connections: Keep connections open between requests to reduce the overhead of establishing new connections.

Compress responses: Use compression techniques like gzip to reduce the size of responses and improve transfer speeds.

Optimize DNS resolution: Ensure your DNS is configured correctly and use DNS prefetching to improve DNS resolution times.

Minimize HTTP requests: Combine CSS and JavaScript files, and inline critical CSS to reduce the number of HTTP requests.

Use a Content Delivery Network (CDN): Distribute static assets closer to users to reduce latency.

Optimize TCP/IP settings: Adjust TCP/IP settings, such as window size and timeout values, to improve network performance.

Consider HTTP/2: If your server and clients support HTTP/2, enable it to improve performance.

Example: Using Keep-Alive Connections

Perl

```perl
use Mojo::UserAgent;

my $ua = Mojo::UserAgent->new;
$ua->options(keep_alive => 1);

$ua->get('https://example.com')->then(sub {
    # ...
});
```


Additional Tips

Monitor network performance: Use tools like `netstat` and `tcpdump` to monitor network traffic and identify bottlenecks.

Test on different networks: Test your application on various network conditions to ensure it performs well in different environments.

Consider using a load balancer: Distribute traffic across multiple servers to improve scalability and reduce load on individual servers.

By implementing these techniques, you can significantly improve the network performance of your Mojo web applications and provide a better user experience.

Chapter 10: Advanced Mojo Use Cases

10.1 Building Real-Time Chat Applications with Mojo

Mojo's WebSocket support provides a powerful foundation for building real-time chat applications. By leveraging WebSockets, you can create interactive and dynamic chat experiences.

Key Components

Mojo::WebSocket::Server: Creates a WebSocket server.

Mojo::WebSocket::Client: Creates a WebSocket client.

Data structures: Store chat messages and user information.

Client-side logic: Implement client-side logic using JavaScript to handle user interactions and display messages.

Steps to Build a Chat Application

Create a WebSocket server: Use `Mojo::WebSocket::Server` to create a WebSocket server that listens for incoming connections.

Handle connections: When a client connects, store the connection in a data structure.

Handle messages: When a client sends a message, broadcast it to all connected clients.

Implement client-side logic: Use JavaScript to create the chat interface, handle user input, and send/receive messages.

Example: A Simple Chat Application

Server-side:

Perl

```perl
use Mojo::WebSocket::Server;

my $server = Mojo::WebSocket::Server->new(
    listen => 'localhost:8080',
    on_connect => sub {
        my $self = shift;
        my $ws = $self->peer;
        # Store the connection
        push @clients, $ws;
        $ws->on_message(sub {
            my $self = shift;
            my $message = $self->data;
            # Broadcast the message to all
clients
            for my $client (@clients) {
                $client->send($message);
            }
        });
    }
);

$server->start;
```

Client-side:

JavaScript

```javascript
const ws = new WebSocket('ws://localhost:8080');
```

```javascript
ws.onmessage = (event) => {
    const message = event.data;
    // Update the chat interface
};

document.getElementById('send-button').addEventLi
stener('click', () => {
                        const      message      =
document.getElementById('message-input').value;
    ws.send(message);
});
```

Additional Features

User authentication: Implement user authentication to ensure only authorized users can participate in the chat.

Private messaging: Allow users to send private messages to specific recipients.

Chat rooms: Create different chat rooms for different topics or groups.

Message history: Store message history to allow users to view past messages.

Real-time notifications: Send notifications to users when they receive new messages.

By following these steps and incorporating additional features, you can build robust and engaging real-time chat applications using Mojo.

10.2 Developing Microservices Architectures with Mojo

Microservices architecture is a popular approach that breaks down large applications into smaller, independent services that communicate with each other via APIs. Mojo can be an excellent choice for building microservices due to its lightweight nature, asynchronous capabilities, and integration with various technologies.

Key Considerations for Microservices Architecture

Service boundaries: Clearly define the boundaries of each microservice based on business capabilities or technical concerns.

Communication protocols: Choose appropriate communication protocols, such as HTTP, gRPC, or WebSockets, based on your requirements.

Service discovery: Implement mechanisms to discover and locate services within your architecture.

Service mesh: Consider using a service mesh like Istio to manage service-to-service communication.

Data management: Decide how to manage data across microservices, such as using a shared database or decentralized data management.

Building Microservices with Mojo

Create individual services: Develop each microservice as a separate Mojo application.

Define APIs: Define clear RESTful or gRPC APIs for each microservice.

Use asynchronous communication: Leverage Mojo's asynchronous features to handle concurrent requests efficiently.

Implement service discovery: Use tools like Consul or Eureka to discover and locate services within your architecture.

Consider using a service mesh: A service mesh can provide features like load balancing, traffic management, and security.

Example: A Simple Microservices Architecture

Service 1 (User Service):

Perl

```perl
use Mojo::Application;

my $app = Mojo::Application->new;

$app->get('/users/:id', sub {
    my $self = shift;
    my $id = $self->req->param('id');
    # Retrieve user data from the database
    my $user = get_user($id);
    $self->res->json($user);
});

$app->start;
```

Service 2 (Product Service):

Perl

```perl
use Mojo::Application;
```

```perl
my $app = Mojo::Application->new;

$app->get('/products/:id', sub {
    my $self = shift;
    my $id = $self->req->param('id');
    # Retrieve product data from the database
    my $product = get_product($id);
    $self->res->json($product);
});

$app->start;
```

Client:

JavaScript

```javascript
fetch('http://user-service/users/1')
    .then(response => response.json())
    .then(user => {

fetch(`http://product-service/products/${user.pro
duct_id}`)
            .then(response => response.json())
            .then(product => {
                // Process user and product data
            });
    });
```

Additional Considerations

Testing: Thoroughly test each microservice in isolation and as part of the overall architecture.

Monitoring: Monitor the health and performance of your microservices.

Security: Implement appropriate security measures to protect your microservices.

Deployment: Choose a suitable deployment strategy, such as containerization or cloud-native platforms.

By following these guidelines and leveraging Mojo's capabilities, you can effectively build microservices architectures that are scalable, resilient, and maintainable.

10.3 Creating Custom Web Frameworks on Top of Mojo

Mojo's modular architecture and flexibility make it an excellent foundation for building custom web frameworks tailored to specific needs. By extending Mojo's core components and adding custom features, you can create powerful and flexible frameworks.

Key Steps

Define the framework's scope: Determine the specific features and functionalities you want your framework to provide.

Create a new module: Create a new Perl module for your framework.

Extend Mojo's core components: Extend classes like `Mojo::Application`, `Mojo::Router`, and `Mojo::Template` to add custom functionality.

Define conventions and best practices: Establish conventions and guidelines for using your framework.

Provide a simple API: Create a user-friendly API for interacting with your framework.

Example: A Simple Custom Framework

Perl

```perl
use Mojo::Plugin;

my $plugin = Mojo::Plugin->new(
    name       => 'MyFramework',
    version    => '0.1',
    requires   => ['Mojo'],
    init       => sub {
        my $self = shift;
        $self->app->config(
            template_root => 'templates',
            static_root   => 'static'
        );
    }
);

Mojo->plugin($plugin);
```

Customizing the Framework

Routing conventions: Define custom routing conventions or use a different routing system.

Template engine: Use a different template engine or extend Mojo::Template.

Middleware: Create custom middleware components to add additional functionality.

Database integration: Provide built-in database integration or support for specific databases.

Security features: Implement security features like authentication, authorization, and input validation.

Benefits of Creating a Custom Framework

Tailored to specific needs: Create a framework that perfectly fits your project's requirements.

Increased control: Have full control over the framework's behavior and features.

Reusability: Use your framework in multiple projects.

Learning opportunity: Gain a deeper understanding of Mojo's internals.

Additional Considerations

Maintainability: Ensure your framework is well-documented and easy to maintain.

Community support: Consider building a community around your framework to foster collaboration and support.

Compatibility: Make sure your framework is compatible with other Mojo libraries and tools.

By creating a custom web framework on top of Mojo, you can tailor your development environment to your specific needs and build more efficient and effective applications.

ISBN 9798339464440